POWERFUL LANGUAGE FOR
RELUCTANT LEARNERS
"AN EDUCATOR'S GUIDE"

Jeremiah's Journey from
Reluctant to Renowned Scholar
"A Powerful Memoir"

GARY A. HUGHES

Archway Publishing books may be ordered
through booksellers or by contacting:

Archway Publishing
1663 Liberty Drive
Bloomington, IN 47403
www.archwaypublishing.com
1 (888) 242-5904

ISBN: 978-1-4808-8749-7 (sc)
ISBN: 978-1-4808-8750-3 (e)

Library of Congress Control Number: 2020902074

Print information available on the last page.

Archway Publishing rev. date: 2/25/2020

Contents

Acknowledgments

I want to acknowledge the following people for inspiring me to share my knowledge. I will start with my parents: Rosalie Hughes, Will Hughes, and Andrea Phillips Hughes. They have poured into me time and time again in a plethora of ways. There is not a day that goes by that we don't talk, and I thank God for them. I would also like to thank all my family and friends for all your support, advice, and encouragement throughout this writing process.

Jeremiah definitely would not be in the position of success today without his mother, Lori Stevenson. She is a constant, nurturing stabilizer in his life who has and still goes beyond the call of duty to create a complete and fulfilled life for him.

Lastly, this book would not be in your possession if weren't for Jeremiah Hughes. Thank you Jeremiah, for allowing me to share some of your early academic challenges to the world. Your academic development and growth allowed me to understand why having empathy as an educator is needed for maximum development of all students.

Introduction

When I decided to step in the classroom as a provisional teacher in 2000, I would have never guessed that twenty years later I would be writing a book about my experiences as a teacher and parent. I will never forget what Principal Bruce Tyler told me early in my first year as a teacher: "Mr. Hughes, the students naturally like you, so use that to your advantage in the classroom." Mr. Tyler was basically telling me that my students would work hard for me because they liked me. I didn't realize it back then but as I reflect today, I realize that I was building genuine relationships with students.

My first year students didn't just walk in my classroom on the first day and immediately like me, as much as I would like to think so. As the years went by, I quietly began to grow a reputation for building relationships with "at risk" and challenging students. My first milestone challenge came in 2006, when Principal Mark King asked me to teach an elective class for at risk and challenging students who were two grades or more below reading level. When Mr. King—now Dr. King—first asked me to take on this task, I was hesitant. I just wanted to continue teaching general education middle school English classes. Mr. King told me that I was the only English teacher in the building who could motivate these children to focus on becoming better readers. To make a long story short, I was able to move 88 percent of these students at least one grade level up in reading.

I began teaching high school English a few years later, where again I was asked to teach a special group of reluctant learners who failed an English course and were repeating the class, and were known as "English recovery students." It was during this time that I began to do extensive reflective thinking about engaging at risk and challenging students in the classroom. During the same time period, while decluttering my house, I stumbled upon a book in my basement that I had never read: *"Positive Words, Powerful Results,* by Hal Urban. I resonated with Hal Urban's principles in this book, which relate to how words can affirm and convey high expectations of students in positive tones. These words build and support positive self-esteem in students, which produces a high-quality educational experience for all students. This book prompted me to create an education workshop titled "Using Powerful Language During Instruction to Increase the Academic Achievement of Reluctant Learners."

The workshop is highlighted by my passionate testimonies of the importance of what I call "powerful language," which motivates and engages all students. I currently travel the country, presenting this educational workshop, which has reinvigorated me and strengthened my focus on reluctant learners—and it has done the same for a thousand or more educators all over the United States. I truly understand why my mentor, Sophia Mallett, always reminds me that "teaching is not a career; it's a calling. One has to be called to do this tireless and feverishly, to see the results of the calling."

The purpose of this book is to increase awareness of the impact our spoken words have on our reluctant learners, assess how powerful words celebrate and affirm student academic life, and showcase preventative and intervention strategies for reluctant learners.

Chapter 1

Who Is a Reluctant Learner?

There are various forms of reluctant learners. I choose to categorize my reluctant learners into three groups.

Group 1 consists of students who have mental processing/functioning issues. These students are typically serviced in special education and have IEPs (individualized education programs), which provide academic accommodations for the student to be successful in the classroom.

Group 2 consists of students who do not have IEPs but are performing below grade level, which inhibits academic success in the classroom. These students do not have learning disabilities but may perform below grade level for one or more reasons. A performance that is below grade level may stem from reasons such as little or no academic support from parents/guardians. Underperforming students may have experienced one academic year with a low-performing teacher; therefore, essential skills needed for the next grade or level of academics, were not obtained by the student.

Group 3 consists of students who are performing on grade level or above grade level. These students may be bored and are not challenged in the classroom. Sometimes these students may be reluctant if they encounter a subject that is too difficult for them. This reluctance could stem from ineffective teaching or a teacher who is challenging and sets standards too high for students to meet or achieve.

My reluctant learner, Jeremiah Hughes, straddled the fence between Group 2 and Group 3. Jeremiah is my son. It was promising early in his life when his infant mind decided he would walk at nine months. His education started well at First Adventure Early Learning Center in Landover, Maryland. He was the only two-year-old in his class that was potty-trained. However, his mother thought it would be best to transfer Jeremiah to another preschool after about a year and a half because of some issues we felt were overlooked by his teachers, as well as swelling classroom sizes at First Adventure Early Learning Center. This transfer was a mistake, because Jeremiah was put out of three early learning centers after leaving First Adventure. Thank God he was allowed to return back to First Adventure, where there was love, structure, and understanding of the whole child. I can't say honestly that Jeremiah was a reluctant learner at this point, since he was so young; however, the First Adventure Early Learning Center staff chose to engage kids with options that the three other schools were not willing to consider.

Hughes Helpful Hint: Sometimes educators have to go beyond the script and find other options if they truly want to make a difference!

Chapter 2

Four Reasons Students Are Reluctant to Learn

There are four major reasons why students are reluctant to learn: (1) the school or subject is not relevant/important to the student; (2) the student fears failure; (3) the student lacks trust in the teacher; and (4) the student has emotional disabilities or suffers from a form of mental instability.

Lack of Relevance

Some students may feel the subject matter at hand is not important, and therefore, the matter is not relevant to them. Students on the elementary level may not be mature enough to understand why it is important to know multiplication facts (without using the calculator). So they may think, "Why go home and study?" Students on the secondary level may not understand why it is important to know how to use an adverb in a sentence. "How will this benefit me in the future?" a secondary student may ask.

For many learners in the twenty-first century, everything about school seems archaic, from the way the day is structured, to the type of assignments they are given, to the policies and procedures in the classroom. The disconnect between "school stuff" and "real life" can be even more dramatic for traditionally underrepresented students in schools that are dominated by the majority culture and are vastly different from the students' home experiences. When reluctant learners cannot see the value in the subject matter in terms of their own lives, lack of relevance leads to disengagement in the classroom.

For students like my son Jeremiah, a lack of relevance leads to boredom. I can vividly remember Jeremiah's kindergarten teacher explaining to me that Jeremiah walked up to her desk and touched everything on it. I asked her if it occurred to her that he was probably just trying to learn something through what educators call kinesthetic learning. In her defense, Jeremiah should not have been at her desk, trying to touch her stuff; however, I'm pretty sure sitting still at a table for at least an hour and focusing did not appeal to a five-year-old.

I have had countless debates with educators who feel that preschoolers and kindergartners should be in an all-day, traditional learning atmosphere. Many of these children are still very baby-like and should be given multiple opportunities to play and have kinesthetic learning opportunities to keep learning relevant. It's amazing how educators want these babies sitting for an hour or longer at a time; yet as adults they cannot sit and focus for an hour or longer at a time. Even for older children, sitting in class and learning in ways that are often linear and passive can seem like a long, slow trudge.

Learners in the twenty-first century typically spend their out-of-school hours engaging in multiple tasks at the same time or participating in activities like swimming and gaming, which provide constant stimulation, escalating challenges, and immediate gratification. If reluctant learners cannot see the relevance of what they are learning or how they are being asked to learn, they will not sustain interest or investment in classroom lessons.

Fear of Failure

Students who have a fear of failure believe teachers and parents have unreasonable expectations for academic success. When these students believe they can't make the goal, they simply refuse to try. These students would rather be chastised for not making the effort than be branded "stupid" for trying and failing. These reluctant learners may see classmates or siblings succeeding easily. When they compare their own stumbling efforts, they come up short. Teachers usually try to tell these students they will be satisfied if they put forth their best effort, but these students are not easily convinced. These reluctant learners refuse to try because it is less damaging to their egos than to try to achieve results that might not be satisfactory. Classroom investment is always a gamble to even the best students. There is no guarantee that hard work will translate into academic success, paying attention during a lesson will lead to instant understanding, or critical reading of *To Kill a Mockingbird* will lead to enjoyment. The negative feelings and repercussions reluctant learners associate with failure can make investment seem like an even worse bet.

Reluctant learners who fear failure disengage for multiple reasons, depending on the student. Some students have a history of failure, and the idea of more failure can be so disappointing that they won't even attempt an assignment. The sad part is these students may have access to resources to help them complete an assignment and still may not even start the assignment. Jeremiah was this very student at times! If he felt like he wouldn't be successful at completing an assignment, he wouldn't even start. On a good day he might put his name on the paper, but nothing else.

Other reluctant learners fear failure because they don't understand how to use resources to obtain success in the classroom. Fear of failure also comes in the form of Group 3—that is, students who do not have a history of failure, but finally encounter a subject and/or teacher that presents rigorous coursework and challenges. A great effort is now required from the student, which leads to students shutting down mentally to avoid the embarrassment of not knowing.

Students who typically fear failure are quick to disengage in the classroom because of what Dr. Carol Dweck, the author of *Mindset,* calls a "fixed mindset." Dweck believes strongly that students have one of two predominant mindsets: they believe intelligence is fixed, meaning there is nothing they can do to get smarter, or they believe that intelligence is elastic, meaning they can grow more intelligent through effective efforts ("growth mindset"). Most reluctant learners have a fixed mindset.

Lack of Trust

Author and educational guru, Dr. Robyn Jackson once stated, "Sometimes students are waiting to see whether you will invest in them before they choose to invest in you." I firmly believe this! Since I have been teaching English recovery (students who are repeating an English course) on the high school level, there is one common element I have noticed about most of my students. They enter my class on the first day of school with a huge amount of distrust toward me. I usually spend the first three to four weeks of school trying to convince them that I have their best interests at heart. It is very evident that they have sat in classes where no real investment has been made in them in a personal way.

I remember the time Jeremiah was so fed up with school during his third-grade year that he just refused to go to school one day. I knew he was struggling in school and he didn't like his teacher. I decided to sit in on his class. I realized that this seasoned teacher only truly invested in certain students, and Jeremiah was not one of them. Yes, Jeremiah did have some academic issues along with misbehavior, but true investment from his third-grade teacher could have helped him so much. After I realized his third-grade year was going down the drain, I wrote the principal and pleaded with her to transfer him to the third-grade class right next door. The principal was hesitant at first to approve the transfer; however, after two more letters from me, she approved the transfer. Jeremiah's new third-grade teacher invested in him right away. The first investment she made was that she expressed to him everything she liked about him and how he would be an asset to her class. (This teacher was very familiar with Jeremiah because he had spent a good amount of time in her class while in time-out). Jeremiah wasn't perfect, but he had a much better year with this teacher. The best part about it was he now loved going to school every day. It's amazing what true academic investment can do for reluctant scholars!

I know it can be tough to try to help students, and they may consistently resist your efforts; however, students believe at some point the teacher will eventually give up trying—and this is exactly what the reluctant learner wants. These students don't want to invest in you, because they don't value you. They don't believe that you can or will help them become successful because in their eyes you care nothing about them as individuals. Why would a student want to make an investment in your class?

Emotionally Disabled or (Not mentally ready for class)

I teach at a school that has a "Transition" program for students that have "IEP's and each student's main disability is "emotionally disabled." These students have teachers who are certified and trained to teach this population and also provide them with crisis intervention therapy when needed. I have been teaching general education English classes for twenty years now, and it seems like I am experiencing more and more students who suffer from some degree of emotional instability. I'm quite sure other general educators have the same reality. It can be as harsh as a seventeen old female foster child who is in class acting out because she still suffers from abandonment issues stemming from her biological mother, who is strung out on drugs. There is also the case of the fourteen-year-old male student who can't focus in class because he has been challenged to a fight via Twitter, which will happen in the bathroom at the next change of classes. Lastly, there is the fifteen-year-old female student who has sent inappropriate pictures to her boyfriend's cell phone, only to receive a text from a friend during your class that states her inappropriate pictures have gone viral on Instagram. The last thing these students want to do is learn when experiencing a mental crisis, which certainly qualifies them as "reluctant."

There are many more reasons why students in preschool, elementary school, middle school, and high school may be emotionally disabled in the classroom. One characteristic that these students may all have in common is their inability to focus on learning in the classroom when emotions are flared up. I'm quite sure there are some students who for many reasons have not been identified as emotionally disabled and are sitting in general education classrooms. Students who obviously suffer from emotional instability to the degree that their responsibility as a student is nonexistent should be reported to administration for the proper consideration of special education services. The Individuals with Disabilities Education Act (IDEA) requires that special education and related services be made available free of charge to every eligible child with a disability, including preschoolers. These services are specially designed to address the child's individual needs associated with the disability—in this case, emotionally disabled, as defined by IDEA (and further specified by states). In the 2017-2018 school year, more than 380,000 children with emotional challenges received these services to address their individual needs related to emotional instability. This type of reluctant learner can be the most challenging to teach.

Chapter 3

Address the Reluctance, and Bring the Reluctant Learner Out

I'm sure educators all over the world would like answers on how to bring out reluctant leaners! As educators we have power every day with students and reluctant learners. What we say that is positive or negative can have a lasting impact in their lives. We all remember the teacher or adult who told us something positive and it was an impactful statement that we will never forget; the same goes for the teacher or adult who told us something negative we will never forget. As educators we need to be cognizant of what we say to students, especially when we are frustrated with reluctant learners.

I was a very good math student until I entered Pre-Algebra in seventh grade. I averaged a C in this class and was placed in a general math class as an eighth grader. When I started high school, as a ninth grader, it didn't take long for me to know that I would struggle in Algebra I. My teacher would teach a lesson, answer a few questions, and go sit at his desk and read the newspaper for the rest of the class. If you asked him any questions after he finished teaching the lesson, he would get irritated, answer the question as fast as he could, and then go back to reading his newspaper. He would also threaten students with failure and make comments about particular students going to summer school while laughing.

I ended up being one of the students who had to attend summer school. However, Mr. Charles Ross opened up a whole new world of learning to me in summer school during his Algebra I class. His repetition of stating the same powerful language every class period eventually became therapy to my ears. He would talk almost like he was singing. Mr. Ross entered the class everyday stating, "Okay, class, let's warrrrm up!" He would give us one or two problems for the warm-up activity. After working out the problem for us and presenting us with the answer, he would sing out, "And it's just that simple!" He would then sing, "Don't you love math? Isn't math wonderful?" Mr. Charles Ross would repeat this powerful language every class. After about two weeks of summer school, my classmates and I believed it was "just that simple." We "loved math," and we believed "math was wonderful." It is important to add that Mr. Ross was a very good teacher, and he was very knowledgeable of his content. He taught in a methodical way, and his teaching steps were consistent and clear. He remained positive at all times, and even when we didn't understand something, he remained patient. His patience was the key to my success in his Algebra I summer school class. I also had him two years later for Algebra II, and I was successful in that class as well.

Let's now address the importance of relevance. Dr. Robyn Jackson states the way to address students' resistance is by clarifying personal relevance. These students deserve to understand why completing assignments and meeting classroom standards are important to them specifically. All lesson plans for student learning should be created to be relatable to students' personal lives. This will not always be easy to do; however, we must find creative ways to make learning relevant.

I vividly remember teaching eighth-grade English as a third-year teacher when one of my students by the name of Bernard asked me a question. I was in the middle of teaching vocabulary and Bernard blurted out, "Mr. Hughes, why do we have to learn all these big words?" I immediately thought about who Bernard was as a young person. I knew he lived in a tough, urban neighborhood, and I was very aware of his environment. More importantly, he was very aware of his environment. I also knew that I had a good relationship with Bernard, so I posed a scenario to him to make learning vocabulary words relevant in his personal life.

I said, "Bernard if you are ever charged with a crime and have to attend court, you will have a lawyer, a prosecutor, and a judge discussing your case. They will be using BIG WORDS and if you don't know what they are talking about, you could end up with an outcome you didn't expect, simply because your vocabulary isn't extensive enough to understand what these three people are talking about. Your fate in court could be determined because of your lack of vocabulary, which is the same as lack of knowledge."

Bernard looked at me, satisfied with my reply to his answer, and simply said, "Okay." Bernard never questioned me again about the lessons I taught. I made learning relevant to him!

Jeremiah questioned in his own mind the legitimacy of education in his early elementary school days. One of the most impactful breakthroughs that we discovered about Jeremiah was his love for learning about the presidents of the United States. My family started buying books for Jeremiah to read, which all related to politics. In the middle of his fourth-grade year, I transferred Jeremiah to Skyline Elementary School in Morningside, Maryland. It was in this school building where Jeremiah's transformation began to take place. Principal Mark Dennison took Jeremiah directly under his wing and made him a relevant student. Mr. Dennison noticed Jeremiah's struggle to read and personally put him in his own "drop everything and read group," which met in Mr. Dennison's office daily for thirty minutes. Principal Dennison also encouraged Jeremiah's love for politics through restorative conversations in which he connected learning in the classroom to success in politics for the future. Learning was finally made relevant for Jeremiah, and he began to transform into a more productive student!

Hughes Helpful Hint: Despite how students may behave, they all have goals of some kind; they all want to be something more than who they are now.

Let's now address fear of failure. Dr. Jackson says resilience is the ability to bounce back from failure. In order for students to attempt difficult work or take risks in the classroom, they need to feel that there is some hope of them being successful. I remember being in parent conferences for Jeremiah during his primary years, and his teachers would bring in work samples to show his mother and me. Sometimes more than half of his assignments would simply have his name on the paper and nothing else. A few of his assignments had evidence of where he did start, but then he didn't even get halfway through completing the assignment. I quickly came to the conclusion that if Jeremiah did not feel he could be successful on the assignment at hand, then most of the time he wouldn't even start. As parents we were very frustrated and disappointed. I was never the parent to put all the blame on the teacher, especially since I am a teacher myself; however, looking back on the situation, I wish Jeremiah's primary teachers had a resiliency plan for him on those days when he decided he would shut down because he decided the tasks were challenging to him. At no point should a student ever be shut down in the classroom. There must be a contingency plan for these individual students.

Dr. Linda Albert, the author of *Cooperative Discipline* created a concept called the "three C's," which stands for "capable, contributing, and connecting." Teachers' goals for reluctant learners should be that these students experience the three C's throughout classroom lessons. Some reluctant learners may not be able to experience all of the three C's, however, they should experience two out of the three and at the minimum one out of three. You need to be creative with how reluctant learners will operate in the three C's. I remember a time when I was teaching a workshop, and I discussed the value of the implementation of the three C's. One of the participants in the workshop asked me how I have students connect in the classroom. My quick reply was that you should start off with saying "Good morning" when a student enters the classroom each day. It seems basic, but this is a great way to connect with reluctant learners every morning. A simple, genuine greeting makes them feel welcome.

The three C's are not just for instructional purposes in the classroom. They also help to establish healthy and positive relationships with reluctant learners, thus decreasing their anxiety of failure during challenging tasks. The three C's don't always have to happen directly inside the classroom. For example, I remember when Jeremiah was asked to be a member of the morning announcements team at Skyline Elementary School. He was still a work in progress at the time but the opportunity to take on this task helped build his confidence back in the classroom as a student. He was able to feel capable, contributing, and connected during his experience as a member of the morning announcement team. I admit it is sometimes difficult to make a student capable, however, I think most reluctant learners can be contributing and connected in some form, shape, or fashion at all times in the classroom. For example, any child can help staple papers for you or any child can help you tidy up the classroom and put books back in order on the book shelf.

Since I currently teach English to ninth and tenth

grade repeaters, I am well aware of the fact that most of them will walk in my classroom fearing failure on the first day of school. I first taught this special group of reluctant learners in the fall of 2015. I remember vividly how they came into class feeling defeated about the previous year. These ninth grade repeaters began to discuss among each other reasons why they failed English 9 the year before. Some of the more verbal students began to ask questions about the class, in particular questioning my style of teaching and my expectations. It was during this dialogue in 2015 that I sensed they feared failure—and it was only the first day of school. As I began my formal introduction of myself, I had to inform them that it was my intent for everyone to pass the class. I included that I believed in their academic abilities, despite what happened in the past. I also added that, with their cooperation at all times, I would do my best to teach them and work hard for their success. This powerful language began to ease their minds and bring them down to earth. This was the start of building resilience in order to bounce these students back from the previous year's failure. This was also the start of creating a much needed trust with the students.

Let's address lack of trust. Dr. Robyn Jackson says if you want students to invest in your classroom, you must invest in them first. Only when students realize that you are not going to give up on them and that you genuinely care about their progress will they begin to invest in you. As I mentioned in Chapter Two, Jeremiah was fed up with school at the start of the third grade and woke up one morning and refused to go to school. Jeremiah's initial third grade teacher did not invest in him, which made

Jeremiah not trust her. Since Jeremiah had a reputation of being "bad" in school since kindergarten, this particular seasoned teacher decided she was going to be the big bad teacher who would be time enough for him. In my opinion, she consistently treated him mean, which ultimately broke his spirit and trust for this teacher. It still makes me feel bad to this day that my son woke up at the age of eight years old and did not want to go to school, because of lack of trust in a teacher. Jeremiah had strong parental support, and for this teacher to take matters in her own hands and break his spirit was unacceptable. Anytime there was an issue with him, I was up at the school at the drop of a dime, supporting the teacher, and this is why the teacher's attitude toward him was so disappointing to me. Students who have little or no parental support should not be subjected to this type of ridicule as well.

I also mentioned in Chapter Two, the third grade teacher whose class he was transferred to actually liked Jeremiah and spoke of his academic strengths. He immediately trusted her, which made him work harder and have more success in her class; however, he was still a work in progress. He developed a great relationship with this teacher and his academics improved simply, because of trust.

My current ninth- and tenth-grade repeaters also have a lack of trust in teachers. It never fails that I spend the first two weeks of school trying to convince them to trust me. Since it is a repeater course, most of them come in dejected and/or embarrassed. They then begin to ask me all kinds of questions about the class, such as "Is this class going to be hard?" "Do we have to read novels?" "Do you give homework every night?" They also have side conversations about their previous English teachers who failed them, most of the comments being negative remarks about the teachers. It quickly occurs to me during their conversations with each other that their trust in teachers is slim to none. It is during this time that I have to purposely build them up with words of affirmation. As I mentioned earlier under "fear of failure", I start with expressing to them that it's my goal that every student will pass my class. I state that with their cooperation I will do everything in my power to make them a more than capable student and person. I explain to them that I know they are smart students with unique talents and skills. I explain to them my job is to strengthen their weaknesses and help them perfect their strengths. Lastly, I let them know it is an honor to stand before them as their teacher. These are not magic sentences, but they become magic if I repeat them over and over again, like I typically have to do for the first two weeks of school to earn their trust. My aim with students who lack trust is to invest in them first and make sure they understand that I genuinely care about them as well as their academic progress. Once I have established trust with these students, a great teacher–student relationship begins, which ultimately leads to success for students in the classroom.

Hughes Helpful Hint: Students' investments may seem small at first and not nearly equal to the investment that you have made in them, but over time, they will invest if you demonstrate that you can and want to help them become successful.

Chapter 4

Positive Communication to Engage Reluctant Learners

Know and Pronounce Students' Names Correctly-

For most of us, nothing is more important than our name and this is true for most of our students. Knowing and pronouncing students' names correctly is important for a student's self-esteem, and it shows that we respect them as individuals. Master teachers believe that pronouncing their students' names correctly is paramount to establishing an authentic teacher– to student relationship, especially with our reluctant learners. Learning all of my students' names has always been a priority to me since I began teaching in the year 2000. The easiest way for me to learn my student's names has always been to create a seating chart and then use this chart to call on them. On the first day of class, before I call the roll, I apologize in advance for the mispronunciation of any names. When I do get to a name that I struggle with, I make it a point to practice saying the student's name a few times just to show the student how important their name is to me. Sometime these students prefer that you call them a shorter version of their name or even a nickname. I don't mind this at all, because it actually helps me remember their names however, I will only call them by their nickname if it's classroom appropriate. I do have to keep in mind that some students, unfortunately, are not proud of their names for multiple reasons. For example, I taught a student that hated her last name for personal reasons, so whenever I called her by her first and last name together, it made her really upset. I learned to stop saying her last name and exercised empathy for her feelings; and that made her respect me more as her teacher.

My good friend and former coteacher, Jeff Studds, once said in regards to knowing and pronouncing names correctly, "I told the students that their names are important, and that the first sign of respect I could show them was to pronounce their names correctly." Mr. Studds went on to say that this tells students up front that he intended to treat them with respect and the act of learning how to pronounce names showed his students he intended to listen to them throughout the school year. Imagine how making reluctant learners feel special about their names could strengthen their engagement in the classroom.

Tell the Truth

It is very important to be honest in communication with students. For example, if you say you are going to do something, you must follow through. Please don't mention any type of reward, such as a pizza party for the whole class if you know you may not be able to provide that reward. If your reluctant learners achieve your goal and you can't reward them, you have lost their trust, which can lead to students not trying as hard in your class anymore.

Another way to be honest is to have one-on-one conferences to discuss students' learning levels. I had a student who used to always come to class and use her cell phone to interact with social media, instead of participating in daily lessons. I had the student come to my desk and I explained to this ninth grader that based on the results of her reading placement scores, she was reading on a fourth-grade level and it would be in her best interest to get off the cell phone and pay attention in class. After being honest with this student in a one-on-one conversation this student was shocked to learn this information. She complained that not paying attention was because of her hunger, since it was the last class period of the day. So I went out and periodically purchased granola bars and mini bottled waters for the whole class, just in case there were other students feeling the same. This student started to come to class with a new attitude, because of the honest conversation and maybe even better the anticipation of being nourished by a granola bar and a bottle of water. Oh! And by the way! The student spent less time on the cell phone in class and her reading levels went up! Please be honest with reluctant learners.

Tell Students They Are Valued

Students should always be reminded, by the teacher, that they hold personal value. For example, a positive phone call home is a great way to show value to reluctant learners when they achieve some type of positive status in the classroom that would be out of the norm for them. Examples could be when a student is helpful in class, completes a whole assignment, or has improvement in behavior. Spontaneous praise reports, such as verbal, handwritten, or preprinted words of affirmation, create student value. For example, I have preprinted laminated notes that state "Thank you" and "I appreciate you." These are given to reluctant learners that I notice following directions and trying their best to learn in all kinds of situations in the classroom.

Dr. Carol Dweck stresses the importance of praising efforts and creating spontaneous praise. These are great ways to let students know they are valued!

Use Polite Words, Kind Words, and Positive Tones

Effective communication with reluctant learners starts with words of encouragement. I used to have a poster in my classroom that stated "Sometimes all we need is a little encouragement." Unfortunately, it was misplaced at my school during a summer break some years ago. I wholeheartedly believe in using polite and kind words with positive tones. It seems I always have a few reluctant learners who initially come into my classroom with a chip on their shoulder. They are mad with attitude problems, and some are just out right mean. Nothing does these students better than words of encouragement with polite and kind words along with positive tones.

Some teachers view using polite and kind words as being too nice to students. The thinking is if you are nice to students, they won't respect you, and therefore you will be taken advantage of in your own classroom. I remember the number one advice from veteran teachers to new teachers for classroom management used to be "Don't smile until January." I knew that would not work for me—because I'm always smiling. My students tell me I smile even while I'm mad. I knew at the start of my teaching career that polite and kind words would be my friendly strategy against students, especially challenging students. I frequently use words phrases like "Thank you," "You're welcome," "Yes, sir," and "No, ma'am."

I remember reading a book on the subject of kindness. The book stated that if you use a consistent dialogue of kind words with people in general, you have a great chance of developing a positive relationship with people. This also works with the coldest, most hardhearted, and meanest people we can think of. Of course these people will not instantly fall in love with you, but after consistently using polite and kind words with positive tones, even the toughest reluctant learners will break! They will still be tough on everybody else but you will receive the soft side of this person.

I have had some tough-looking students, in particular boys (most of them are sixteen and seventeen in the ninth grade) who are six feet and taller with tattoos on their necks and faces, along with the rugged attitudes to complement their physical features. However, my consistent and specific use of kind words and actions breaks their hardcore personalities. They eventually transform into well-mannered young children in my classroom. I even found out that using polite and kind words with Jeremiah was more effective than berating him when he made mistakes. One of my seasoned mentor teachers, Ms. Lauvinia Alston, who is now retired, used to always say, "You get more bees with honey!" Get honey from your reluctant learners with polite words, kind words, and positive tones.

Laugh with Students

I have a coworker, Terri Newsome, who was quoted as saying, "A laugh a day keeps the crazy away." I wholeheartedly agree. I personally love to laugh, and I am humorous by nature, so I enjoy light humor and jokes with my students most days. I know some educators are not humorous by nature and don't really care to be with their students however, there are benefits to humor and laughter in the classroom. Light, appropriate jokes with laughter help reluctant learners know that you are actually human. If you are not funny by nature, then tell corny jokes and share funny moments about yourself every now and then. Believe it or not, students will appreciate your attempts at being funny and they would love to hear about funny moments in your life. Some of the funniest moments in my classroom happen when I attempt to use my students' slang words to get their attention. My students fall out laughing and think it's hilarious.

There are also therapeutic benefits of laughter for you and your reluctant learners. Laughter activates and strengthens the immune system. Laughter reduces at least four hormones associated with stress. Laughter provides a "workout" for the diaphragm and increases the body's ability to use oxygen. Laughter relaxes the muscles. Laughter can significantly reduce pain for long periods. Laughter lowers blood pressure and can prevent hypertension. Laughter improves respiration by emptying the lungs completely of the air taken in. Laughter has no negative side effects on the body. Lastly, laughter is available anywhere, without a prescription for free.

One of Jeremiah's favorite elementary school teachers at Skyline Elementary School used to let him tell jokes in her afterschool program, and she built a good relationship with him through humor, which helped him have academic success in her classroom. Take advantage of humor and laughter with your students whenever it's appropriate. It will definitely benefit your health and help you build trusting relationships with your reluctant learners. Trust supports academic success.

Celebrate Students' Accomplishments

Celebrating reluctant learners is a non-negotiable. It must happen, even if we have to create ways to have a celebration. Reluctant learners need to understand that meeting specific guidelines are causes for a celebration. The milestone may not be huge but the growth should be measured and celebrated, and it does not have to always be attached to academics. For example, it could be a celebration or certificate given to the most helpful student of the week. I have given recognition and rewards for similar classroom characteristics unrelated to academics and it actually propelled reluctant learners to strive harder in academics. When you get the reluctant learners motivated to strive harder in academics, you can begin to attach celebrations to milestones of academic achievement.

Most educators and parents of primary age children are familiar with the red, yellow, and green behavior chart. Red means the child had a bad day, yellow means the child had an average day, and green means the child had a good day. Well during most of Jeremiah's kindergarten days, he came home with a red report. One day I asked the teacher if Jeremiah ever did anything the right way and to my surprise, she said, "Yes." I then asked her why Jeremiah came home with red behavior reports most days. She said it was because his good moments were far and few in between. She did state that he sometimes had a better morning than afternoon. So we came up with an idea that the teacher would give Jeremiah two behavior reports for each day: one for the morning and one for the afternoon. So finally Jeremiah finally started getting green reports for the morning or the afternoon, depending upon the day. He did not become perfect by any means but he gradually started having better days because we finally got a chance to celebrate him for having green reports. He even occasionally had green reports for both the morning and the afternoon.

In addition to teaching students who have failed ninth- and tenth-grade English, I teach English to at-risk ninth grade students. These particular ninth grade students are with me, because of one or all the following reasons: low grades in middle school, low attendance in middle school or frequent misbehavior in middle school.

Again, celebration is a must with all of my students. One example of a celebration I have with my students is giving them a pizza party in the middle of the year. In the recovery system at my school, I teach the ninth-grade repeaters English 9 every day for the first and second quarters. If they pass the class during the first and second quarters, they are eligible to take English 10 during the third and fourth quarters. If they pass both English 9 and English 10 through this system, they will have recovered two English credits in one year. This system works the same way for my tenth-grade repeaters, but with English 10 and English 11.

The pizza party in the middle of the year is only for the repeaters who successfully pass quarters one and two and are eligible to move to the next English course. I always announce this anticipated event to the repeater students at the start of the school year, and expectations are made clear as to what they must achieve to attend. I will never forget the first year I had this party for my ninth-grade repeaters. After they were served pizza, soda, and desserts, I distributed laminated paper certificates to the students, which stated "Congratulations for passing from ninth-grade English to tenth-grade English." I did not think this was going to be a big deal but these certificates turned out to be more important than the pizza! The students started running up to me to get their coveted certificates. One student, a seventeen-year-old ninth-grade student, was so excited that he told me he couldn't wait to get home and show this certificate to his mom and hang it up on his bedroom wall. This student explained to me that he had not received any type of recognition of achievement since he was in the second grade. It was at this moment that I truly understood the value in celebrating accomplishments of reluctant learners!

Listen, Smile, and Make Eye Contact While Students Are Talking

Some well-known philosophers believe there is a reason why humans have two ears and only one mouth. The belief is it's more important to listen than it is to talk. This is definitely an important skill set to possess in the classroom with reluctant learners. Listening helps you learn specifics about your reluctant learner, and it helps them build trust in you. The ability to smile and make eye contact while in dialogue with reluctant learners helps them feel secure knowing that you are concerned about who they are in your classroom.

I will never forget one time when I was sitting at my desk in my classroom at the start of the day taking care of multiple tasks. A student came to my desk and began talking to me. I quickly acknowledged the student by looking up and then looking back down at my laptop but I continued listening to her. All of the sudden, she blurted out, "Mr. Hughes, look at me when I'm talking to you!" I did not get offended by her raising her voice, and I actually stopped what I was doing and listened to her. I can't remember what she said to me, so I know it wasn't an emergency conversation; however, it made me realize how important it is to our reluctant learners that we give them our undivided attention when they need it, even if a meeting has to be scheduled with the student. Again, this process builds trust and it helps our reluctant learners feel secure, knowing that you will specifically acknowledge and listen to them in the classroom.

Listening is also important outside of the classroom. Some years ago when I was a middle school teacher, there was a student in my eighth-grade class who was fifteen years old. He was new to our school and he started maybe a month after the start of school. The administration thought it was a good idea to socially promote him to high school in the middle of the year, simply because he looked older than all the other kids. He was not a behavioral problem at all and he was actually a nice, respectful kid.

Since this boy was a special education student, the school had to have an IEP meeting with his mother to make sure his IEP was worded properly for his transition to high school. I was chosen to be at the meeting and represent the IEP team as one of his general education teachers. During the meeting, the special education chairperson announced the name of the high school the student would be attending. Upon hearing the name of the school, the student said, "I don't want to go to that school. I'm beefin' with kids who go to that school." The translation of his statement meant, "I don't want to go that school because there are some guys there that don't like me and they want to physically hurt me." For some reason, nobody in the meeting, including his mother, paid attention to the student's statement. I immediately repeated to the special education chairperson, while looking at his mother what the student had said. The special education chairperson shushed me to be quiet and continued to talk about the next steps to transfer the student out. The mother looked at me briefly and then continued to listen to the special education chairperson. I couldn't believe that nobody was concerned about what this child had said, which meant to me that they were not really listening to him and didn't seem to care. The only goal they had was to get the boy out of the building.

Two weeks later, this fifteen-year-old boy was found dead in a neighborhood across town. He had been shot to death. I don't have a clue why he was killed and I don't know if it had anything to do with the statement he made in his final IEP meeting at our school before he was transferred out. What I do know is that nobody in that meeting took the time to listen to him. If the IEP team had listened to his concerns about attending a high school that he did not want to attend, maybe he could have received some help or advice and he might be still living today. This was a sad ending for a young person who may have lost his life because educators were not listening. Please find time to listen to your students! You may be the listening board and the difference between life and death.

Chapter 5

Powerful Language for Academic Achievement

I recently read an evaluation of one of my recent workshops. One evaluator stated the title of my workshop, "Using Powerful Language during Instruction to Increase the Academic Achievement of Reluctant Learners," was slightly misleading. However, the evaluator stated that it was a workshop full of good information. I'm guessing that this evaluator assumed that the "powerful language" part of the title meant that I would be discussing some type of "rocket science" vocabulary to teach to reluctant learners, which would inspire the students to use these words in their vocabulary in order for them to learn. Or maybe the evaluator thought I was going to give the participants in my workshop some fancy big words or terms that would magically increase the academic achievement of reluctant learners. The latter of the two assumptions is closer to my intent however, the term "powerful language," which may be misleading to some participants does not mean rocket science vocabulary or fancy big words and terms. I define powerful language as encouraging phrases of affirmations that are powerful if consistently stated to reluctant learners.

Here are twenty-one powerful language statements that I use in my classroom for my reluctant learners.

Good morning!/Good afternoon!
Please greet your students every time they enter your classroom. You may be the only adult in their life that actually greets them in a genuine way on a daily basis.

It's good to see you! Students need to know that you are genuinely excited to see them every day.

I'm glad you could make it today!
This is for your students who have attendance issues. Be careful not to make this statement in a sarcastic tone.

You are important to this class! I use this statement for students who are off task and it's great positive encouragement to redirect them back to the class lesson. I once stated this to an off-task student during a formal observation and my administrator loved it! The administrator actually noted it in her comments.

Your success is important to me! I believe in you! This is for your students who sometimes want to give up. If they know you truly believe, they can be successful and they will continue to try.

You're the greatest, like Muhammad Ali! I use this statement when a student really impresses me and they love it.

I'm proud of you! This statement needs no explanation. Your students should hear you say this often, especially if they are giving you their best efforts.

I'm not successful unless you are successful! This is what I say during a one-on-one conference with students who are struggling academically or just not giving a full effort. I truly believe as a teacher you are only fully effective if your weakest student is learning.

I apologize. Apologies from a teacher to a student may be the most powerful statement ever, especially in terms of repairing a teacher–student relationship. For example, if a student misbehaves and I yell at them, I always make sure to go back to the student and apologize for yelling at them. I do tell them that they were wrong but I also acknowledge that I was wrong as well. My mentor Shauna King, author of *School Smart: It's More Than Just Reading and Writing* said the following in regards to apologies "We often justify comments, by saying "I didn't mean it that way" or "That wasn't my intention". While this may be true, it is less important than how the other person is impacted by it. Does having your foot stepped on hurt less if it was an accident? No. At those moments, if your intentions were truly not to cause harm or hurt, the appropriate response is not an explanation, but an apology." Some of my best relationships with my most challenging students were formed and sustained through apologies.

Excuse me for my mistake and thank you "Jeremiah" for correcting me.

Admitting to a student that you have made a mistake is an honor of humbleness. I remember the irritation and sometimes embarrassment of making a mistake in front of students and then being called on it by students. If you let your ego get in the way, a debate against students will follow; and this happened a few times with me. Now, when I make an occasional mistake, such as spelling a word wrong or calculating a test grade incorrectly I am quick to acknowledge my mistake with dignity and students respect my honesty. It's also a great time to remind students that you are human!

I get excited when you are learning! There is nothing like your students seeing and hearing that you are excited about them excelling academically.

I love it when a plan comes together! You may or may not be a fan of the eighties TV sitcom series *The A-Team* but this catch phrase used by the character Hannibal is frequently used by me, when my students are engaged and interactive in the lesson of the day. It shows my students that I am enthusiastic about their understanding and participation of the lesson.

What do I need to do to make you successful? Instead of pleading and begging a student to do a better job in the classroom, pose this question and make them feel like you are up for suggestions. You would be surprised at the responses students give you that will help you become a better teacher. This question also lets students know you care about their academic progress.

Thank you for your cooperation! This is a simple statement of kindness to confirm to students that you appreciate them following directions.

Thank you for getting started. This is for your students that struggle to start assignments. Be careful not to make this statement in a sarcastic tone.

Thank you for turning in your assignment. This is another simple statement of kindness to confirm to students that you appreciate them listening. I will never forget the time I thanked a student for turning in his assignment and he looked at a classmate and stated he couldn't believe I was thanking him for turning his assignment. I thought that was so amusing.

I appreciate you! This statement goes without saying and I probably tell this statement to random students one hundred times a day!

I noticed your improvement today! If you want to make a student smile, who has been struggling and finally shows academic improvement, this is the best statement in the world.

You worked hard today! Every student loves this statement, whether they consistently work hard or they are improving in the classroom—and it doesn't take long to say.

You had a good day! This statement goes without saying. It is another statement that all students love to hear!

I see you! I love to yell this to individual students who really surprise me with great and unexpected academic achievements.

I know many educators have used some of these phrases of encouragement and affirmation for years and years. However, have these statements been powerful phrases for reluctant learners? The following quote made by Haim Ginott makes the meaning of powerful language very clear to me: "I have come to the frightening conclusion that I am the decisive element in the classroom. It's my personal approach that creates the climate ... As a teacher, I possess a tremendous power to make a child's life miserable or joyous. I can be a tool of torture or an instrument of inspiration."

No teacher displayed this philosophy better than Mrs. Baynes, who was Jeremiah's teacher in the fourth grade. Her powerful language was the start of his transformation as a student, and the former "bad" kid eventually became the senior class president of Bowie High School for the class of 2015. Jeremiah is currently a senior at a university in the state of Maryland, majoring in political science and upon graduation he will attend law school. These achievements were all founded on powerful language for a reluctant learner. Jeremiah's journey became easier when he encountered educators that used powerful language while teaching him. Powerful language starts engagement, and if used consistently it leads to renowned academic achievement for all students!

Printed in the United States
By Bookmasters